W9-APO-307

MVP BOOKS

AVAILABLE NOW
from Lerner Publishing Services!

The *On the Hardwood* series:

Boston Celtics	Miami Heat
Brooklyn Nets	Minnesota Timberwolves
Chicago Bulls	New York Knicks
Dallas Mavericks	Oklahoma City Thunder
Houston Rockets	Philadelphia 76ers
Indiana Pacers	Portland Trail Blazers
Los Angeles Clippers	San Antonio Spurs
Los Angeles Lakers	Utah Jazz

COMING SOON!

Additional titles in
the *On the Hardwood* series:

Atlanta Hawks
Cleveland Cavaliers
Denver Nuggets
Detroit Pistons
Golden State Warriors
Memphis Grizzlies
Phoenix Suns
Washington Wizards

To Order • www.lernerbooks.com • 800-328-4929 • fax 800-332-1132

ON THE HARDWOOD

UTAH JAZZ

J.M. SKOGEN

On the Hardwood: Utah Jazz

MVP Books
2255 Calle Clara
La Jolla, CA 92037

MVP Books is an imprint of Book Buddy Digital Media, Inc., 42982 Osgood Road, Fremont, CA 94539

MVP Books publications may be purchased for
educational, business, or sales promotional use.

Cover and layout design by Jana Ramsay
Copyedited by Susan Sylvia
Photos by Getty Images

ISBN: 978-1-61570-849-9 (Library Binding)
ISBN: 978-1-61570-833-8 (Soft Cover)

Table of Contents

Chapter 1
JAZZ'S FIRST STAR

When most sports fans think about Utah, they immediately think of the Jazz. This NBA team has been in Utah since 1979, and is the 18th oldest NBA franchise in the league. It is also the longest standing Major League sports team in the state. So it is understandable that "Jazz" brings to mind bright purple jerseys, and heroes like John Stockton and Karl Malone. But if you stop to consider this name, Utah is not a state that most people would associate with jazz music. Utah summons images of breathtaking natural wonders, like the red earth formations of Arches National Park. Folk music—passed down from the settlers who carved out a new life in this pioneer state—might be a good soundtrack for Utah's rugged beauty. But jazz?

To get to the bottom of this mysterious name, you must think of an entirely different part of the country. Picture yourself in the muggy heat of Louisiana, walking down Bourbon Street. The smell of Cajun food fills the air, and jazz music drifts along the Mississippi

Arches National Park in Utah.

River. That's right, the Utah Jazz was originally the New Orleans Jazz.

The New Orleans Jazz, established in 1974, was only in Louisiana for five short years before moving to Utah. During that time, the team stayed off the NBA's radar in most respects. They were not playoff contenders, and they did not rise up to challenge the great teams of that era. But they could boast one thing that no other team possessed: the showmanship of "Pistol" Pete Maravich.

Pete Maravich was not someone you would pick out of a line of basketball players to be a star. His 6' 5" frame was slender, and he had shaggy brown hair in a time when many players were clean cut. Maravich's signature style included "lucky" gym socks that were always falling down around his ankles. However, despite appearances, Maravich

New Orleans Jazz player, Fred Boyd, scores during a 1975 game.

was not only one of the greatest basketball players of all time, he also knew how to put on a show like none other.

As a child, Pete Maravich ate, slept, and breathed basketball. According to *New York Times* reporter Pete Thamel: "When Pete Maravich was growing up, he would dribble a basketball out the car window as the family drove into town. He would even take a ball with him to the movie theater, sit in an aisle seat and dribble throughout the show." Maravich went on to play college basketball at Louisiana State University, where he emerged as one of the best players ever.

Pistol Pete Maravich, with the help of his "lucky" gym socks, was a star at Louisiana State University.

His average was a staggering 44.2 points per game—a record that is still unbroken 42 years later. As stunning as that record is on its own,

A Deserving Honor
In 1987, at age 39, Pete Maravich was the youngest person to ever be inducted into the Basketball Hall of Fame.

Pistol Pete played for the Atlanta Hawks before being traded to the New Orleans Jazz.

it is simply mind-blowing when you remember that the three-point shot was not even established yet. All of Maravich's soaring shots across the court were only worth two points.

After a whirlwind of attention from both the ABA and NBA, Maravich was ultimately drafted by the NBA's Altanta Hawks in 1970. With the Hawks, Maravich averaged between 19.3 and 27.7 points per game over his first four years. Not only was he brimming with talent and potential, but Pistol Pete knew how to draw a crowd with his entertaining playing style. In 1974, when the New Orleans Jazz were looking for a ready-made star to lead their new team, they looked no further than Maravich. After trading

Atlanta a king's ransom in the NBA world—two players and four draft picks, including the first pick in the 1974 NBA Draft—Pistol Pete came home to Louisiana.

Back when the NBA still allowed nicknames on jerseys, Pete Maravich wore "Pistol Pete" on his back. He was called "Pistol" because he had a deadly aim with the ball, and he was bullet-quick. Even his father, who was also his coach at Louisiana State, called him "Pistol." He played like a magician, or a circus performer: never taking a straight shot when he could make it exciting. Maravich was the master of behind

Don't Miss!
When Pete Maravich was just 11 years old, he made 500 free throws in a row.

the back, between the legs, and no-look passes. Broadcaster Chris Hern commented on Pistol Pete's playing style: "He was like a great singer, with a style all his own, a

Pistol Pete performs one of his "magic acts" with the ball.

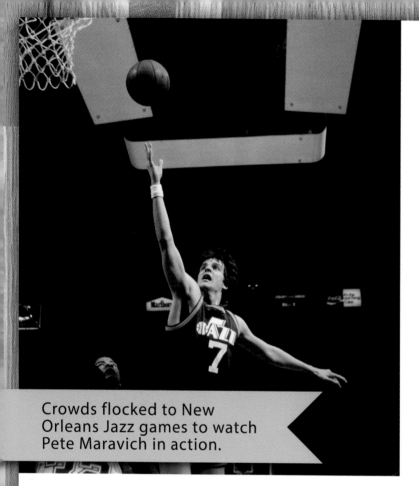

Crowds flocked to New Orleans Jazz games to watch Pete Maravich in action.

Maravich. He drew in crowds who—watching Maravich perform in his Mardi Gras purple, gold, and green jersey—felt like the carnival had come to town.

However, for all of Pistol Pete's talent and style—he scored an incredible 31.1 points per game in 1976-77—the New Orleans Jazz were not the contenders in the league. In fact, they never once made the playoffs. There were many reasons why the team did not immediately prosper. Some critics point to poor financial and business decisions off the court. Others say that, while Maravich

pacing that was different, a flair for the unusual." Jazz, a type of music known for improvisation and a lively spirit, seemed to perfectly represent

A Man to Remember

Utah retired "Pistol" Pete Maravich's #7 jersey in 1985. In 2003, the New Orleans Hornets also retired the #7 jersey in his honor.

was unquestionably a star, he did not always play as part of a team. Then the unthinkable happened. Maravich suffered a terrible knee injury during the 1977-78 season. He was performing one of his "tricks"—a high-in-the-air, through-the-legs pass. When he landed, something tore in his knee. This moment changed Maravich's life forever. He had to miss a number of games, and when he returned, much of his grace on the court had vanished. However, even while dealing with constant knee issues, Pistol's overwhelming talent never truly faded. Maravich made his fifth career All Star appearance in 1978-79.

In 1979, after struggling financially in New Orleans, the team announced that they were moving

The moon and the snow-dusted hills rise above Salt Lake City's skyline.

Moses Malone drives to the net for the Utah Stars of the ABA. The Stars were Utah's first basketball team.

to Salt Lake City, Utah. The owners of the Jazz apparently thought the people of Utah could use some music in their lives, and decided to keep the name, and the Mardi Gras colors. Though this was Utah's first NBA team, Salt Lake City was actually quite familiar with professional basketball. From 1970 to 1975, SLC had been home to the Stars—an ABA team that had folded just before the ABA-NBA merger. The Stars had been very popular, so when the Jazz arrived, there was already a huge fan base to welcome them.

Though Pete Maravich was not the force on the court that he once was, and actually retired from basketball in 1980, the Jazz never forgot their beloved player, and first star. In 1985, they held a ceremony to retire his #7 jersey—the first uniform to ever be retired by the Jazz. During the ceremony, they showed a video of Maravich's "greatest hits." Utah fans looked on with wonder and pride as Pistol Pete moved with an unearthly speed and showman's flair across the court.

Just one season prior to this 1985 ceremony, some pretty great things were happening for the Utah Jazz. They had just made their first postseason appearance in 1984. Led by forward-guard Adrian Dantley, they went all the way to the Western Conference Semifinals. Then, Utah picked a little

Though John Stockton did not look like a star at first, he became one of the greatest NBA players of all time.

known rookie named John Stockton in the 1984 NBA Draft. Fans did not suspect that this unassuming 6' 1", 175-pound player was the first half of a duo who would change the face of their franchise forever.

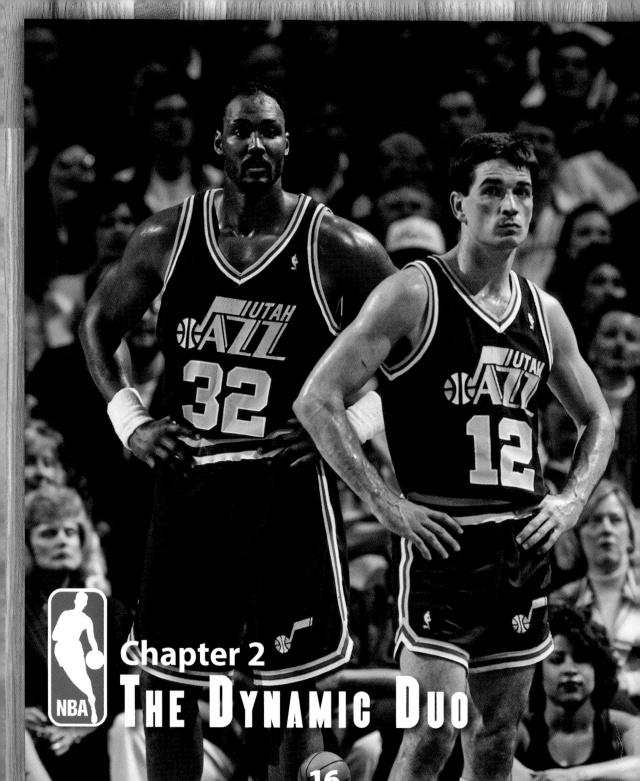

Chapter 2
THE DYNAMIC DUO

When Utah Jazz fans heard who their team had chosen with their #16 pick in the 1984 NBA Draft, they were not happy. In fact, upon hearing the name "John Stockton" over the loudspeakers at the Draft in New York, they booed. Jerry Sloan, who was the head coach of the Utah Jazz from 1988 to 2011, recalled: "That's right, they did boo him. They yelled: 'Who is this guy? Where's he from?' He did, of course, eventually change that opinion." Not only did John Stockton prove his worth during his first few seasons, but over the course of his 19-year career with the Jazz, he became an NBA legend.

John Stockton, with his slender build and "boy next door" smile, did not look very intimidating. And he certainly didn't look like a player who would lead the NBA in career assists and steals by a landslide margin. Stockton was always content to stay out of the spotlight, even if it meant that fans (and other teams) underestimated his abilities. During a game,

John Stockton was smaller than most players, but he more than held his own.

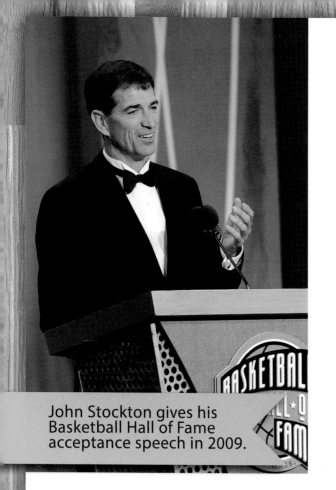

John Stockton gives his Basketball Hall of Fame acceptance speech in 2009.

the world that he would never back down from a challenge. Growing up in Spokane, a small city in Eastern Washington, John Stockton had one main competitor—his older, and much larger, brother Steve. When John Stockton was inducted into the Naismith Basketball Hall of Fame in 2009, he recalled learning the ropes against his brother: "I wasn't even the best player in my own house. My brother Steve boasts a record of about 1,000-1 in bloody driveway battles. That one victory, though, ended all the games. That's my one claim to fame with Steve."

Stockton stayed in his hometown for college, where he attended little known Gonzaga University on an athletic scholarship. During his senior year, John Stockton was

he usually looked to set up his teammates, who could then be the stars when the ball swished through the net. However, just because he did not seek out attention did not mean that John Stockton was willing to be anything less than the best.

Early in life, Stockton showed

briefly forced onto center stage when three other starting players were out with injuries. He carried the team to a winning season, and walked away with the league's MVP award. Stockton emerged as the first Bulldog to ever record more than 1,000 points and 500 assists, and the first to be drafted into the NBA. Though at first glance Jazz fans thought this small player lacked star appeal, they soon discovered that John Stockton played with enough ferocity and determination to rival anyone in the NBA.

Indeed, John Stockton quietly showed Utah his strength and usefulness during his rookie year. Though he started in only five games during the

1984-85 season, Stockton led the Jazz with 415 assists (172 more assists than any other Jazz player that season), and was third in steals. However, it wasn't until 1987-88—when

John Stockton flies past Laker Kareem Abdul-Jabbar for a layup.

Malone's strength and speed were the perfect addition to the Utah Jazz roster.

Stockton was finally a consistent starter—that his already fantastic play soared to another level. That season, he recorded an astonishing 1,128 assists. And the man on the receiving end of many of those assists? Karl Malone.

Malone grew up in the small town of Summerfield, Louisiana, and was the youngest of eight children. Tall and strong, Malone always looked the part of the star athlete. However, when it was time to start his college career one thing held him back—his grades. Taking his mother's ad-vice, Malone went to college—Louisiana Tech—but sat out from basketball his first year to buckle down and study. The next year, when he was academically eligible to play, Malone put his school on the map for college basketball. He led his team to its first two NCAA appearances, and earned the nickname, "The Mailman," because he always delivered. When Malone was chosen by the Jazz as the 13th pick in the 1985 NBA Draft, the fans' reaction to the news was quite different than with Stockton. When they made the announcement at Madison Square Garden, that the Jazz was going to "bring a Mailman to Utah," the crowd exploded.

From 1987 to 2003, the greatest words a Jazz fan could hear were "Stockton to Malone." The grace of their play—when Stockton tossed the ball effortlessly to the net, and Malone was there to slam it home—was like an elaborate dance. In appearance, however, you could not find two more opposite images then the slight Stockton, and 6' 9", 259-pound Karl Malone. Rather than calmly smiling after making a great play like Stockton did, Malone enthusiastically

Go Bulldogs!
Though Stockton went to Gonzaga, and Malone went to Louisiana Tech, their college mascots were both the Bulldogs.

celebrated many of his baskets—jumping up and down, hands in the air, high-fiving everyone within reach.

During the nearly two decades

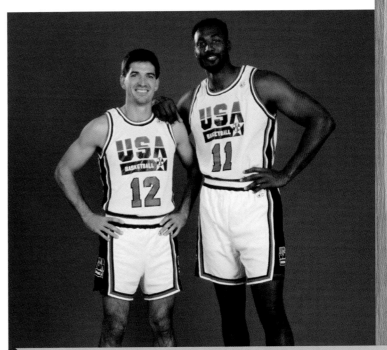

In 1992, Stockton and Malone joined the U.S. Olympic Dream Team in Barcelona. They came home with gold medals.

Stockton and Malone run a pick and roll play against the Chicago Bulls during the 1998 NBA Finals.

they played together, Stockton and Malone took one of the most basic moves in basketball, the pick and roll, and perfected it. The pick and roll is a play where one offensive

Immortalized

There are statues of both John Stockton and Karl Malone outside of Utah's EnergySolutions Arena.

player sets a pick: blocking or "screening" a defensive player, so that the offensive player with the ball can get around him. Then the person who set the pick "rolls" away, and is now open for a pass. When done correctly, this move is very hard to defend, because either the player with the ball will be open for a shot, or the one who screened the defender will be open for a pass.

Stockton and Malone negotiated this technique with a skill that comes from perfect teamwork. They are still the top example of flawless execution in almost any article about the pick and roll. Malone, with his huge frame, was ideal for screening and taking hits, while Stockton had a surgeon's hands when it came to passing. Fans never knew just how Stockton was going to pass to Malone, and almost felt like they were watching a magic trick when the ball suddenly popped into the air, and into Malone's firm grip. However, Stockton was also tough enough to go up against much larger players, and wasn't afraid to get a little roughed up by setting a pick himself.

For all their different attributes, the things Stockton and Malone had in common—impeccable work ethic, durability, and determination—helped to create a legacy of greatness that would forever link these two players in the minds of their fans. Together, they made the whole country stop and take notice of the team from Salt Lake City, and made sure the Jazz were playoff contenders every single season. They also brought back the showmanship that had been the hallmark of Pistol Pete's playing style. However, while Pete Maravich was a one-man show, Stockton and Malone were one of the league's greatest dynamic duos.

Chapter 3
ALMOST CHAMPIONS

1997 WESTERN

In the spring of 1997, Utah had basketball fever. After rooting for their team through a fantastic 64-18 regular season, Jazz fans were thrilled to see them easily dispatch the competition in the playoffs. First, Stockton and Malone helped clinch a blowout 3-0 series against the Los Angeles Clippers. Next, the Jazz defeated the Los Angeles Lakers four games to one. Utah had been to the Western Conference Finals three of the past five years, but the fans had never before seen such utter control and dominance from their team. If Utah could keep up this unstoppable momentum, and beat the Houston Rockets in the Western Conference Finals, they would move

The Utah Jazz steamrolled the L.A. Lakers in the 1997 Western Conference Semifinals.

on to the NBA Finals for the first time in team history.

Though the Jazz had made it through the first two rounds of the playoffs easily, Utah knew that the Houston Rockets would provide stiff competition. Houston had recently won NBA Championships in 1994

Red, White and Blue Jerseys

Stockton and Malone teamed up with other NBA stars a second time during the 1996 Summer Olympics.

and 1995. In the process, they had knocked the Jazz out of the running in the 1994 Western Conference Finals, and in the first round of the 1995 playoffs. Houston also boasted such stars as Clyde Drexer,

and Charles Barkley—talented players who had been teammates of Stockton and Malone's on the 1992 Dream Team.

Salt Lake City came out in purple and gold to root for their team during the first two home games against the Rockets, cheering Utah to victory. However, Houston took the next two games in Texas, tying up the series. Then, after the Jazz responded with a Game 5 win in Utah's Delta Center, Salt Lake City was once again filled with hope. When Utah sent their team back to Texas for Game 6, they had one goal in mind: return home Western Conference Champions.

By 1997, Stockton and

Charles Barkley and Karl Malone square off during Game 4 of the 1997 Western Conference Finals.

Malone had already collected a stack of NBA honors. Both players had made All-Star game appearances every season since 1989 (Malone since 1988). They also had four Olympic gold medals between them. Commentators were already saying that Stockton and Malone were not only destined for the Hall of Fame, but were two of the 50 best NBA players ever. However, for all of their achievements, John Stockton and Karl Malone had never been to the NBA Finals. As they took the court for Game 6 against Houston, listening to an arena full of people rooting against them, they knew that this was the game that could change their legacies.

Jazz head coach Jeff Sloan calls out a play during the 1997 Western Conference Finals.

It was a close game, as both Utah and Houston desperately tried to take the lead. Fans watching from home, and even Houston fans rooting against him, expected a lot from Malone. And The Mailman delivered—scoring big, and picking rebounds out of the air with ease. But what people didn't expect was that Stockton, who often passed the ball to other players, started making basket after basket himself. However, the Rockets were holding their own, with Charles Barkley determined to make his first NBA Finals appearance with the Rockets, and Clyde the Glide heating up the court with a game-high 33 points.

With 30 seconds to go, the game was all tied up. But then, after two successful free throws from Barkley, the Rockets were leading 100-98. Houston fans, who had been been holding their breath when the game was tied, exploded with cheers. The

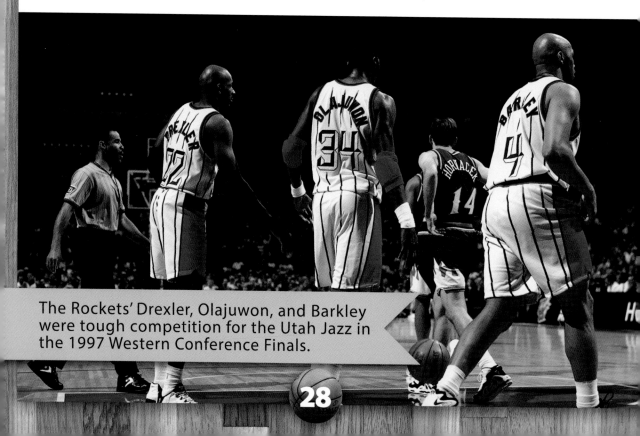

The Rockets' Drexler, Olajuwon, and Barkley were tough competition for the Utah Jazz in the 1997 Western Conference Finals.

Rockets had won two out of the last three Western Conference Finals series, and Houston fully expected to see their team continue this pattern.

When the game clock started again, Stockton caught the inbound. He calmly dribbled to half-court, sizing up his lane to the basket, and then took off. Stockton shouldered his way past bigger men, weaving like a boxer, then launched himself into the air for two points. The crowd gasped in horror when the ball went in. The score was tied once again, 100-100. After 20 more seconds of nail-biting game play—with neither team breaking the tie, the Jazz had the ball

with 2.8 seconds left in the fourth quarter. Commentators wondered who would get the inbound this time. Would powerhouse Malone take the game winning shot? Or would Stockton, who had scored nine points in the last two minutes

John Stockton makes the game winner against the Houston Rockets.

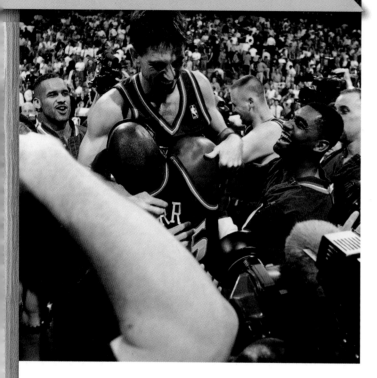

broke away from the huddle of players. He sprinted, wide open, to half-court, and was there to catch the inbounded ball. Stockton took three steps and jumped, shooting a rainbow jump shot through the air towards the basket. Swish. The final score was 103-100, Jazz. The arena instantly filled with disappointed groans and shrieks of surprise.

of the game, be on the receiving end of the ball?

When the teams took the court again, they grouped near the top of the key. Charles Barkley stuck close to Karl Malone—ready to cut him off from the ball. Then, in the blink of a eye, it was John Stockton who

As soon as he saw that the shot was good, normally cool, calm John Stockton leaped into the air, shouting with joy. The rest of the Jazz flooded the court, forming a hugging mass of purple jerseys. And when his team lifted him into the air, Stockton looked weightless.

The Utah Jazz returned to Salt Lake City to find 20,000 people waiting at the airport. After 23 years as a franchise, the Jazz had finally done it—they were Western Conference Champions. Utah celebrated, and prepared to send their team off to face the Chicago Bulls in the NBA Finals. Ultimately, Michael Jordan and his team of reigning champions proved too tough for the Jazz. However, after this amazing season, the whole country knew that Utah was a team to be reckoned with. Also, though Chicago won the NBA Finals, Utah had another mark of distinction that spring. Karl Malone edged out

Karl Malone holds his 1996-97 NBA Most Valuable Player trophy.

Michael Jordan to take home the 1996-97 NBA Most Valuable Player— one of the few honors that Malone had not yet received.

Chapter 4

THE MAN WHO LOVED UTAH

When considering those who have shaped the Utah Jazz over the years, many think of John Stockton, or Coach Jerry Sloan. Indeed, Stockton was as loyal as he was talented—he spent his entire 19-year career in Utah. He was so well respected that in 2003, when he played his final game ever, in the Sacramento Kings' arena, that rival crowd gave him and Malone a standing ovation. Coach Jerry Sloan was also a fixture in SLC. He led the Jazz to 15 straight playoff seasons, two trips to the NBA Finals, and was their coach from 1988 to 2011. This was the longest that anyone had coached one team in the history of the NBA. But it wasn't just a great coach, or a talented set of players, that allowed this team to flourish. At the root of the Jazz's success in Utah stood one man, who on two separate occasions, held the fate of the Utah Jazz in the palm of his hand.

Coach Jerry Sloan was inducted into the Basketball Hall of Fame in 2009... the same year as John Stockton!

Larry Miller, a businessman who earned his first millions in the auto industry, grew up in Salt Lake City. After a rocky childhood, Miller learned that if you wanted something great out of life, you had to make it happen yourself. Early on, Miller developed a deep sense of pride for the beautiful state of Utah. In 1985, when Miller heard that his state's only professional sports team might move to Miami, he was horrified. He thought that the people of Utah deserved better. The only way to prevent the team's departure, it seemed, was to buy half of the franchise himself. At the time, Miller was worth about $4 million, but he needed $8 million to buy into the team. Also, in its 11 years as a franchise, the Jazz had yet to become profitable. The team

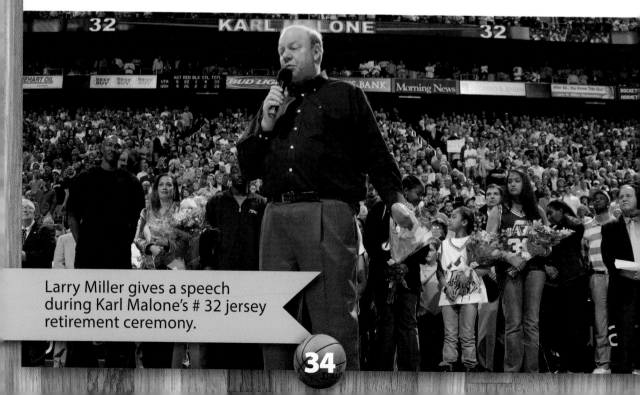

Larry Miller gives a speech during Karl Malone's # 32 jersey retirement ceremony.

was, by many accounts, a bad investment.

Though the numbers were against him, Larry Miller did not give up. He went to different local businesses and banks to try to find financial support. Utah's *Desert News* tells of Miller's determination, stating that Miller actually "crashed a meeting of bankers," to present his case. Miller told the bankers a story to prove his own reliability: "I got my first telephone in my name when I was 12 years old because I was on the phone all the time. My parents had to sign for it, but I had to pay the bill. Since that time, I've been paying bills, and I've never missed a payment on anything in my life. If you can find

Larry Miller presents head coach Jerry Sloan with a basketball in honor of Sloan's 1,000th career win.

a delinquent payment, turn me down. If you can't, make this loan." This heartfelt speech convinced the bankers, and they gave him the loan to save the team.

In the first year after Larry Miller

Hard Work Pays Off

Larry Miller started out as a stock boy for an auto parts store. He later became the 10th largest car dealer in the U.S.

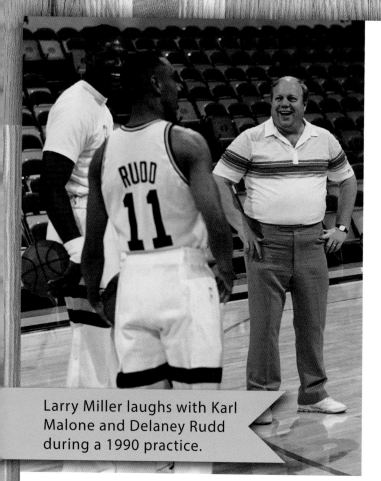

Larry Miller laughs with Karl Malone and Delaney Rudd during a 1990 practice.

Miller wanted to once again keep the Jazz in Utah, he would need to pay $14 million for the second half of the team. Selling his share, however, would not only have wiped away his massive debt from buying half the team in the first place, but he would have made quite a profit. Miller was on the brink of selling, and was about to sign the paperwork that would have allowed Utah's NBA team to move to Minnesota. In fact, the pen was in his hand. But then he stopped. Miller simply couldn't allow his beloved team to leave Utah. To him, the team was as much a part of the state as the beautiful landscape. "Selling the Jazz," Larry

bought the Jazz, he become a very involved owner—he even suited up and practiced with the players. The franchise also started to make money. In 14 months, the franchise had almost doubled in value. At that time, the man who owned the other half of the Jazz decided to sell. If

Miller later said "would be like selling Canyonlands." He bought the rest of the team, and never looked back.

After twice saving the Jazz from moving across the country, Larry Miller took a firm hold of his franchise, and possibly saved it for a third time. Until 1991, the Jazz were playing in an outdated arena. With 12,666 seats, the Salt Palace was the smallest arena in the NBA. It had become clear that, if they didn't do something to increase ticket sales and revenue, the franchise could once again be in financial dire straights. But Miller saw that Salt Lake City was full of fan support. They just

Natural Wonders
Canyonlands, Utah's largest National Park, is full of mesas, river canyons, and other breathtaking natural formations.

needed a bigger space to show their appreciation. So, in 1990, Miller built the Delta Center. This new arena, completed in time for the 1991-92 NBA season, could hold 20,500 fans. It was even later used for the 2002

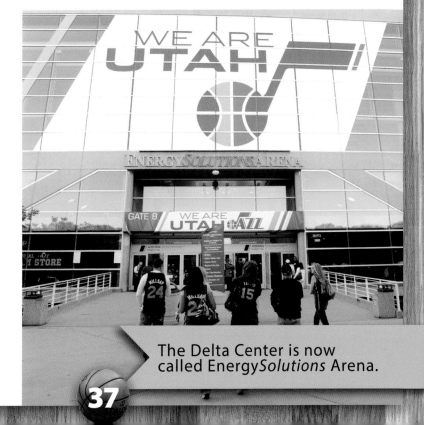

The Delta Center is now called Energy*Solutions* Arena.

Winter Olympics. Once again, the franchise grew in fame, and respectability. Salt Lake City watched two NBA Finals series in their new arena, and saw their beloved team come so close to winning it all.

Unfortunately, though Larry Miller had a great head for business, his health was later a constant struggle. In 2009, after a long fight with Type II Diabetes, he passed away at the age of 64. His family held Larry Miller's viewing and funeral in the place he loved: his arena. The people of Salt Lake City came out in huge numbers to show their respect and sorrow. Doug Robinson describes how, "For six hours, thousands lined up for the viewing at the basketball arena, many of them waiting more than two hours, and at the end of the line Gail [Larry's wife] embraced or shook the hand of every one of them."

Larry Miller's wife Gail, and their son Greg, carry on the Utah Jazz legacy.

The Utah Jazz bow their heads in honor of Larry Miller before a 2009 game.

In all his years as the owner of the Jazz, Larry Miller did not think of the team as a business. Sure, he made excellent business decisions, but to him, the Jazz was a gift to the great state of Utah. The Salt Lake Tribune quoted Larry Miller as he described his purchase of the Jazz: "It was an opportunity, I realized, to give a community and a state that I care a great deal about something that maybe nobody else could give them." At the end of his life, Larry Miller wanted to be remembered, not for his financial accomplishments, but for the love he felt for his home. When he died, those were the words that his wife had inscribed on his headstone: A Man Who Loved Utah.

Chapter 5
A Decade of Change

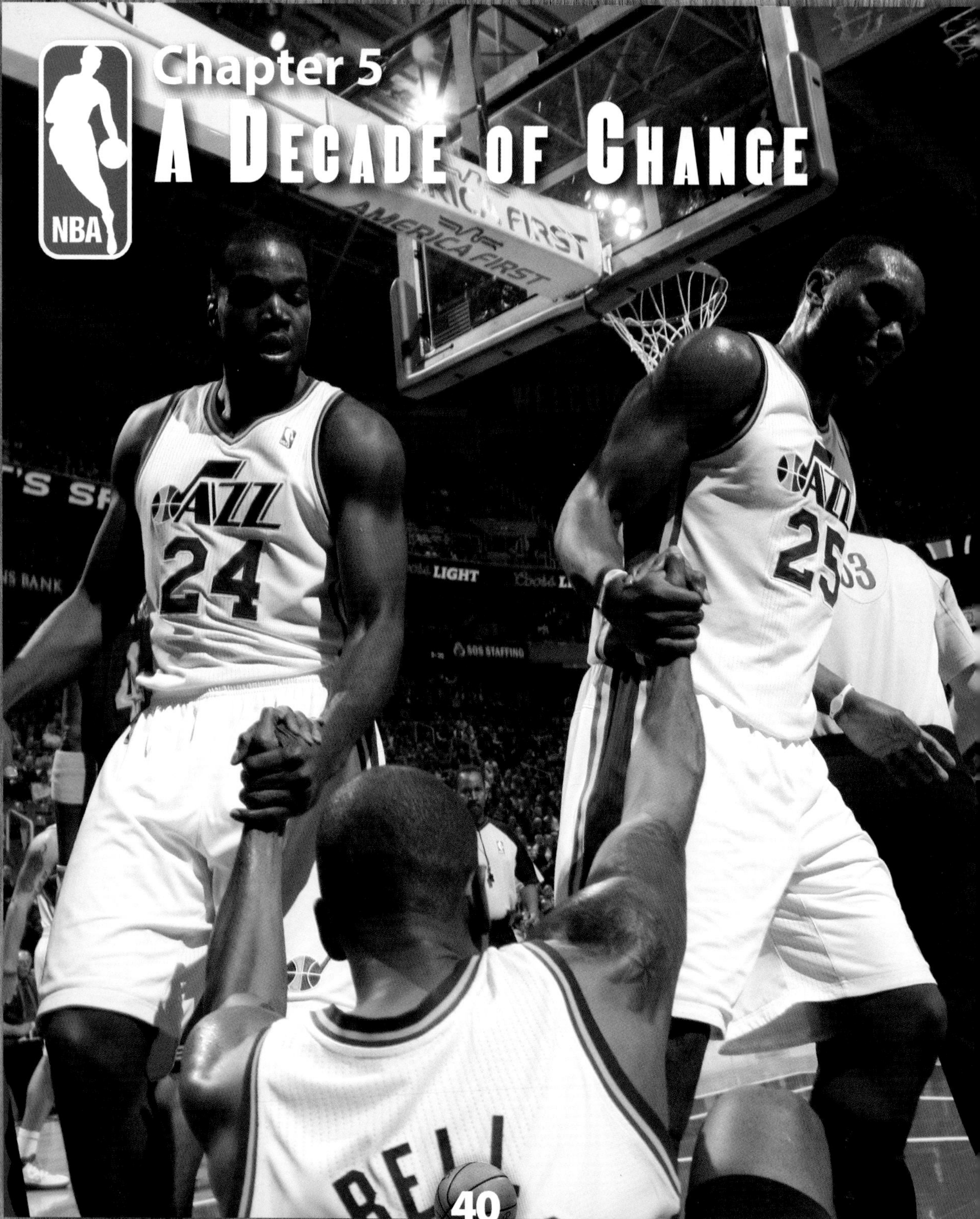

By 2003, there were a few things that Salt Lake City knew for sure about springtime: May was followed by June, and the Utah Jazz would be in the play-offs. Under Coach Jerry Sloan's guidance, the Jazz never once missed the postseason in 20 years. However, all that changed when Utah's most famous Jazzmen left after the 2002-03 season. John Stockton retired, and Karl Malone played his final season with the L.A. Lakers—hoping to finally add NBA Champion to his list of honors. Without their two stars, the Jazz went through some serious growing pains. In 2004, Utah was absent from the postseason for the first time since 1984. When Utah's dry spell continued through 2005,

Deron Williams holds up his brand new Utah Jazz jersey after the 2005 NBA Draft.

the Jazz used their 26-56 regular season slump to nab the 3rd pick in the 2005 NBA Draft.

It was no surprise when the Jazz used that pick to select Deron Williams—a talented point guard from the University of Illinois. During his junior year, Williams helped the Fighting Illini reach the first NCAA

Championship Game in school history. Though they lost to North Carolina, this was still a great accomplishment for the young player. After this success, Williams decided that he was ready to enter the NBA Draft before his senior year. *Sports Illustrated's* Seth Davis ranked Williams as the second-best point guard in the 2005 NBA Draft, and called him a future All-Star.

By Williams' second year with the Jazz, he created quite a buzz in Salt Lake City. Together with top-scoring teammate Carlos Boozer, Williams led the Jazz to a 12-1 start to the 2006-07 season. Following in the footsteps of the Jazz's most famous point guard, Williams notched the highest assist total of any Jazz player since John Stockton.

Williams' comparison to the Jazz legend was only furthered by Carlos Boozer's similarity to Karl Malone. Like Malone, Boozer was huge: a 6' 9," and 250-pound forward.

Carlos Boozer throws down a monster two-handed dunk against the Toronto Raptors.

It also helped that their first names were almost identical: Karl and Carlos. Whenever the announcers called out "Williams to Boozer," fans felt like the spirit of their old dynamic duo was alive on the hardwood. However, as much as Williams and Boozer were flattered to be compared to Jazz legends, they also wanted

Carlos Boozer and Deron Williams take the court before Game 4 of the 2010 Western Conference Quarterfinals.

to make a name for themselves. In 2007, Boozer said: "Deron and I are not trying to walk in [Stockton and Malone's] shoes. They are too big to fill. We have to make our own footprints. We are the face of the organization now."

The Jazz finished out the 2006-07 regular season with a greatly improved 51-31 record, and made the playoffs for the first time since 2003. That year, not only did the Jazz return to the postseason, but

A Global Childhood
Carlos Boozer was born on a military base in West Germany in 1981, but grew up in Juneau, Alaska.

Deron Williams goes up against Chris Andersen of the Denver Nuggets in the 2010 NBA playoffs.

elite—and had a new set of Jazzmen to celebrate.

For the next three years, the Utah Jazz were back to business as usual. They made playoff appearances every season, and kept chasing their long-sought-after NBA Championship. However, in 2011, the Jazz were in for another huge change-up: Coach Sloan's retirement. By 2011, Jerry Sloan had been Utah's coach for more years than some players had been alive. His retirement in the middle of the 2010-11 season—just a few short years after owner Larry Miller's death—seemed to truly mark the end of an era.

Then, just a few weeks after

they went all the way to the Western Conference Finals. There was a new kind of excitement in the air in Salt Lake City, as Utah rejoined the NBA's

Man of Many Skills
When Jerry Sloan played basketball for Evansville College, he also made refrigerators for Whirlpool.

Coach Sloan left, the Jazz traded Deron Williams to the New Jersey Nets. Williams was coming to the end of his contract with the Jazz, and, though Utah would miss their talented point guard, they wanted to build for the future. Utah exchanged Williams—then a two-time All-Star, and 2008 Gold Medalist—for a promising young rookie named Derrick Favors, seasoned point guard Devin Harris, and two future 1st round draft picks.

Though the Jazz endured another rebuilding process without their longtime coach—missing the 2011 playoffs—they were back in postseason contention by 2012. By the start of the 2012-13 season, the Jazz had restructured their roster

Al Jefferson takes a shot against the OKC Thunder in a 2012 game. Paul Millsap waits for the rebound.

Paul Millsap goes to the basket against the Phoenix Suns.

youthful energy, and veteran confidence. Though Jefferson was entering his ninth season in the NBA, he was still quite young—only 27 years old. This was because Jefferson had chosen to skip college, and go straight from high school to the NBA.

Weighing in at 6′8″, 245 lbs, Paul Millsap formed the second part of the team's inside duo. Similar to Utah legend Karl Malone, Paul Millsap grew up in Louisiana and went to Louisiana Tech. Also, like Karl Malone, Paul Millsap was a forward who looked more like a football player. Millsap was drafted by the Jazz in 2006, and seven years later, he was still playing in Utah.

to form a "big man" backbone: Al Jefferson and Paul Millsap. At 6′ 10″ and 289-pounds, Jefferson had certainly earned his nickname "Big Al." Jefferson was the team's powerhouse—he averaged 18.9 points per game after joining the Jazz in 2010. When he took the court, Jefferson gave off a combination of

Even as they rooted for Jefferson and Millsap, many Jazz fans were also looking to the future in the form of Derrick Favors—the 21-year-old rising star who had come to Utah in the Deron Williams trade.

Derrick Favors was one of the Jazz's best players off the bench. Like Jefferson, Favors had started his NBA career early. In 2010, Favors became the fifth player from Georgia Tech to enter the NBA Draft after only one season. During his rookie year, Favors was praised for his athleticism, and ability to move quickly on the court despite his size. It was clear that this 6'10" power

forward had the talent and drive to play more minutes. He averaged just 21.2 minutes per game in the 2011-

Derrick Favors attacks the net in a game against the Minnesota Timberwolves.

Derrick Favors, Al Jefferson, and Paul Millsap are the Utah Jazz's "big men."

12 season. However, with Millsap and Jefferson in the starting lineup, the Jazz already had a lot of "big men" on the court. If potential changes shuffled the lineup, allowing Favors to take more of a leadership role, there was no saying how far this young man's talent could take him.

Through the years, Salt Lake City has watched its team grow into a respected franchise with a storied history. Though the face of the Utah Jazz may change with each passing season, the love and loyalty of their city and fans remains constant. If Utah continues to cultivate a strong, exciting roster, then surely—one day soon—the Jazz will finally hit that last high note, and bring home their long-awaited NBA Championship.

rH4